To Alexa,

Happy Christmas 202

Judge Deb

and the Battle of the Bands

Paul Kerensa

Illustrated by Liz and Kate Pope

A long, **long** time ago,

Deborah was a **judge**;

she made up her mind

and she didn't often **budge**.

She had an eye for talent
and she had an ear for God,
which helped her decide and say
exactly what was what.

From the **palm tree** at her judge's house,

she gave out her **opinions**:

'**Yes** to that' and '**No** to that'

and 'Leave that for my **minions**.'

In fact, so many fans

tried to speak to *wise* Judge Deb,

her friend 'JL' became her bodyguard...

Such a celeb!

Well, not quite *everybody*
came to listen at her tree.
A **naughty** man called Sisera said,
'*I'm* the judge of me!

I'll do *what* I like, to *whom* I like
and make a lot of noise.
No one is the boss of me!
We're Sisera's Boisterous Boyz!'

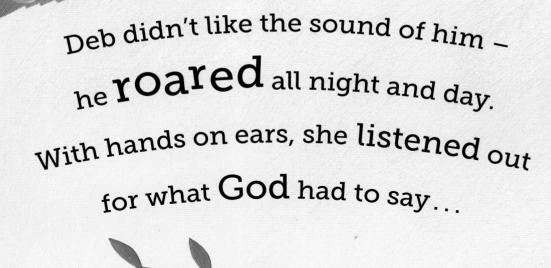

Deb didn't like the sound of him —
he **roared** all night and day.
With hands on ears, she **listened** out
for what **God** had to say...

God told her, 'Fetch that **singing star**,
who tours around these lands.
Barak should face old Sisera...
in a **Battle of the Bands!**'

Barak was quite the **superstar**,
both **talented** and **nice**.
He visited Judge Deborah,
for **wisdom** and **advice**.

'Where next for my **career?**' he asked.

So Deb revealed God's plans:

'A **sing-off** against Sisera! . . .

and bring **ten thousand fans**.'

Barak invited everyone –

TEN THOUSAND clicked 'Attending'!

'I'm nervous, though,' he said,

'and so ... *one more* invite I'm sending ...

I can't do this without you, Deb!

I need you there, backstage,

to cheer me on, to cheer him gone,

to end his rude rampage.'

Deb said, 'I'll gladly join you,
but know that when all's done,
the victory won't be yours to boast –
the women will have won!

And any song to come from this,
your name will be **eclipsed**.
"**Judge Deb**" is sure to be the name
on **everybody's lips.**'

Barak agreed – but, on arriving,

didn't like his chances.

Onstage *strutted* **Sisera** with

nine hundred backing **dancers!**

A **loud** guitar, a drum with **flames**,
a golden *motorbike*...
From where **Barak** was standing,
Sisera **rocked** the mic.

'Bit noisy,' groaned the crowd,
as Sisera finished strumming.
Backstage, Barak was worried –
butterflies were in his tummy.

The Judge then nudged,
'This is the day, given to you by God!
He's warmed the crowd – go loud and proud!'
She gave Barak a prod.

Barak stepped out in faith and, then...
his nerves just disappeared.
He sang his first long note...
'Yeaaaah!' – the audience all cheered!

He sang, he played, he plinked, he plonked,
he grooved, he growled, he howled.
Judge Deb looked on and grinned and grinned...
Sisera stared and scowled.

'That does it!' shouted Sisera,
'They want a *real* rock star!'
He ran back to the microphone,
clutching his guitar.

'My Boisterous Boyz behind me?
Let's make some noise!' he blared,
but heard no sound, so turned around –
his Boyz had run home scared.

Sisera felt **alone** – he didn't know
God like Barak did,
so dancing offstage quickly
was his new **retreating** tactic.

Bodyguard JL stood by the door marked
'Venue exit'
and kicked him out the concert –
Sisera *yelped* and then he **pegged** it.

Barak remembered Deborah's words,
that 'women will have won'...
and, sure enough, JL had shut out
Sisera – stopped his fun.

'Ladies and gents!' Barak announced,
'Sisera's gone for ever!
To sing us out, the real winners,
JL and JUDGE DEBORAH!!!'

Deborah took the microphone,

she gave it a quick tap and

said 'I love *you! God does too!*

Now . . . here's how it happened.'

They sang of Sisera's **Boisterous Boyz,**

who'd **terrorized** the locals,

till she and JL **saved** the day!

(Barak sang backing **vocals.**)

They **sang** until the **sun** went down,

till **singing** turned to **yawning**.

The **land** would be more **peaceful**

when they **woke** up in the **morning**.

So whatever song is yours to sing,
sing it **proud** and **strong**!
And know that **God** is centre stage –
he's been there all along.

For Phoebe
I rocked her and now she rocks me

First published in Great Britain in 2020

Society for Promoting Christian Knowledge
36 Causton Street, London SW1P 4ST
www.spck.org.uk

British Library Cataloguing-in-Publication Data
A catalogue record for this book is avaliable from the British Library

ISBN 978–0–281–08412–8

1 3 5 7 9 10 8 6 4 2

Interior design and typesetting by Anna Lubecka, Banana Bear Books
Printed by China

Produced on paper from sustainable forests